Time is Never Planned

Anna Flint

Presentation by *BookLeaf Publishing*

Web: www.bookleafpub.com

E-mail: info@bookleafpub.com

ISBN : 9789357447966

First edition 2021

Athena

I didn't know her when she whispered in my ear,
All persuasion and mesmeric.
The information to be pasted to my mind.
Dive into the bottle and win baby, win.
In a few short hours we'll be dancing through
traffic.
Soaking in a second skin of early morning rain.
Pulled up and tranced out with our faces
gleaming.
The thumping of the whole world's vibes
running through our veins.
Drink up darling, memories will fade
And we'll pray together at the altar of chemical
drop.
A second chance lives in this bottle so give in.
We, like lost ghosts, swim.

Mind of a Traveller

A landscape so flat,
But your curves are seen,
Heading further into your features.
No road to travel on,
We create our own on your gravel.
No sign of life but us,
You intrigue us to see more,
Show us everything.
We, the travellers love you,
Leaving our footprints in your breath.

As Simple as a Smile

We fight for money, land or greed,
Do we succeed in just creating enemies?
We are good people,
Maybe even friends.
There's war and anger,
But try bringing us together,
It's peace and laughter.
We all have opinions, but some are mutual,
These good memories are shared.
And these people are friends not enemies.
No fighting is required for happiness.

Her Township Smile

A smile, so simple, so beautiful,
It's a curve on a person's face.
One girl, a young girl,
She possesses this smile,
The beautiful curve,
An unfortunate girl,
Yet a happy girl.
We all possess such beauty,
But she wore it best.
A house of wood,
No water, no health,
But she was happy,
Stunningly happy,
And her facial curve,
Showed such beauty.

I Bless the Rains

Natural beauty in one place.
Hurry boy it's waiting there for you,
Wind in my hair, my face.
Off the beaten track.
Do the things we never had,
The feeling I'm alive.
Wonderful species and nature beside.
Long forgotten words,
His motocross girl.
Excitement in each direction you turn.
Frightened of the thing that I've become,
Exhilaration as I plummet.
Nature working wonders.
Drag me away from you,
A parachute to save my life.

An Overseas Shake

We take on this road,
Leaving our hand signs and footprints
For them to cherish.
Their smile growing as they see us;
May only be for a second,
But a second they remember.
Now a foreign friend they have gained.
A second together worth a lifetime.
Their tiny hands respond
With their face responding more.
Knowing our eyes will never meet again
We head further down the road
To leave our hand signs and footprints.

One Day

One day when the sun burns down,
And my skin is turning golden.
They'll be a place: small village or town
Where my heart will here be stolen.

One day when the rain kisses my skin,
And the life around me grows.
The voices will expand from within
And joy will come with suns and snows.

One day when winter is coming,
And the white blanket is lay.
The nature around will be numbing
Yet till a path to follow for the way.

One day I'll take a climb,
Into the shallows or the deep.
Here is when it's my time.
My time to take that leap.

The Next Train

We hopped on and off, here and there,
The scenery around us forever changing.
The destination to only we knew where,
And the conversations which we were
exchanging
The different languages, we took them in.
All the cultures and events we could now begin.

Different countries and cities pass us by,
We took every opportunity to go and explore.
We greeted all with our hellos and goodbyes.
Feeling enlightened to keep going for more
We joined in with the languages and
conversations,
And made our way along to our next station.

The colours and scents overwhelm our senses
Pleasant or not we fell further in love.
Those cities and towns; a range of addresses
Many memories we gained, a gift from above.
As we stumbled down the different lanes,
It was now time to board our next train.

A Fork in the Road

In life you are given chances.
Chances to pick a path.
This path will decide your future:
Simplicity or adventure?

The path to your left,
A simple looking friend.
So straight and so simple,
No obstacles lie ahead.

The path now to your right,
A more undesirable stranger.
Deep, dark and destructive.
How dare I think to tread?

I'm judging by their looks,
When the outcome is unknown.
Do I want to choose the simple?
Or experience the unimaginable?

The choice is mine now.
One step will change my life.
Breathe in. Count down.
3... 2... 1...

Abuelos

You told me to do my best,
The lyrics for my life ahead.
The words not made in jest,
But in love and feeling instead.

Always striving to do my best,
The motivation to make you proud.
Uttering words that came from your chest,
The ones spoken with serenity yet loud.

You knew I'd do my best,
Throughout everything you had hope,
Whether it was that race or that test,
You helped me to cope.

You told me to do my best,
And that was all I could do.
And I love the words you expressed
For it was your "I love you".

Amigo

Dancing in circles, we play and we run,
Feeling untouchable as we chase the sun.
Our hands are held as the glow slowly fades,
We're laughing and falling onto the grass blades.
The ground is soft and tickles our face,
Does this have to end, it's the perfect place?

As the sun slipped away, so did our grins,
In our favourite spot the silence wins.
Your fingers round mine, I held them tight.
No fear in our minds, not even a slight.
The monsters can come, the fiction can't harm.
We know if they do, we've got the alarm.

The moon was now up and we laid so still,
Our imagination wild and causing a thrill.
We don't have long now until this ends
We both know the finale and always stay
friends.
As we sit up there's the monster we feared.
Another day over and I disappeared.

Daddy's Little Girl

The girl she is,
A product of you
An ambitious and hardworking girl.

You gave her the world,
You're a hero in her eyes
And couldn't do any wrong.

She remembers wrapping her hands
Around your little finger
But now you're wrapped around hers.

You tell her she can be anything
In this big and scary world
But she only wants to make you proud.

The flashback of singing
A little out of tune to the radio
Appears in her head.

You were driving her,
With glances to one another
as you sang your hearts out.

She's driving herself now,

Thoughts of you never leave her mind
As she takes her next adventure.

You're an aspiration,
The man who hung the moon
And she was daddy's little girl.

Guidepost

You taught me to be happy,
Filling my senses with love.
There was nothing I couldn't be,
Surrounded by smiles and laughs.

Without you, I'd be nothing
Receiving my looks and life's blood.
Our bond was never breaking.
Thick as thieves the two of us.

I believed I had the power.
Able to create anything I could.
With all the people and flowers,
You inspired my childhood.

You told me to be anything,
When all I wanted was to be you.
Brave, caring and happy
You taught me to be me.

To My Best Friend

If she could see herself through our eyes
She'd see there's never any lies.
Her face a unique piece of art,
With beauty in every mark.

The song that we call laughter
Sounds like heaven out of her.
She's a girl to call a friend
Which I hope never comes to end.

For we met when it was fall
And shared our laughter through it all.
And during our infancy we played
Whether it be sunshine or in shade.

When we grew up together,
Who knew if we'd have forever.
And although our life was bending
It gave me hope it wasn't ending.

For without her here around me,
I don't know where I'd be.
And even when she's not around
She will still make me proud.

An Irritating Superhero

Kind is your nature
And inspirational is your presence.
Yet irritating is your nature
And provoking is your presence.
An irritating superhero
Who'll come and change the day,
I don't think I would like you any other way.

Trusting is your person
And happiness is your laughter.
Yet impatient is your person
And sarcastic is your laughter.
An irritating superhero
Who knows how to make me smile,
Maybe not straight away or even in a while.

Thoughtful is your energy
And selfless is your speech.
Yet bothersome is your energy
And mockery is your speech.
An irritating superhero
Who will never let me doubt,

And one I would struggle to try and be without.

The Screams of Hands

Do you remember being a child?
Everything new and exciting,
Bright colours and smiles.
A new friend to add to the collection
Each and every week.

Dreams were big and adventurous,
You'd be king of the country
Or going for picnics with your teddies.
You'd want to be an astronaut or a doctor,
Teacher or ballerina, all doors were open.

However, the doors have started closing
And your dreams become nightmares.
No teddy to protect you now,
You are on your own.
With a new darkness to add to the collection,
Each and every week.

I Sometimes Imagine This

I read in a book that it is not just the earth that is
dying,
But actually the universe itself.
Going back to where it originally came from.
The animals are dead and land itself.
Last year, everyone I knew, knew someone
that'd died.
One language dies every four months.
My phone, as I write, is dying.
So I sometimes imagine this:
The last person with the last word
Of the very last language,
On what is now her rare and miraculous tongue,
Is thankful that, at last, there is nothing left to
say.

Don't Blink

Caked in make-up I rush for the bus
Huffing and puffing my mum makes a fuss
No time for breakfast so I eat some crisps
Can't be bothered with assembly but my teacher
insists
I sit there bored, stultified
The teacher asks questions. I'm trying to hide
I'm walking down the corridor to the lesson I
hate
Strolling as slow as I can, I'm already late
'Is there any point now?' I think in my head
Before I know I'm out the gates, I've already left
Results day comes and I'm not surprised,
My friends are chuffed I have expressionless
eyes
I don't take it to heart because I don't really care
Sat at lunch with my friends, out the window I
stare
The following day my kids wake me up
Making breakfast and hovering, I feel so grown
up
Its their first day at school, it's gone so fast
"Pick us up after school!" I hear one of the them
ask

I make up all the beds, though it'll soon be
bedtime
As a stay-at-home mum I have plenty of time
My husband's at work, won't be back till late
The house will be tidy, food on his plate
Is this the way life's supposed to be?
No social life, jobless, mother of three.
The following day, what's that sound?
It's the house phone ringing, grandkids coming
round
I roll out of bed, put my slippers on
Looking behind me, I can't believe he's gone
My man of 84 died last week
He had pains in his arms and legs and feet
A heart attack took him, though he lived a good
life
I hope I'll do him proud being his 82-year-old
wife
Looking back at the years, I've missed so much
Forgot to live my life, it was such a rush
Time is uncertain and I'm really not sure
Where my whole life went, now treading on
death's door
I'm old and weak, nothing left to give
My family surrounds me, as I no longer live
For I, just get by every day
Struggling to do anything I live in dismay
I'm blue in the lips and I lay there cold

Wishing I made more of my life, I say goodbye
to my soul.